English
made easy

Preschool
Ages 3–5
Rhyming

Author Su Hurrell

Certificate

Congratulations to ....
(write your name here)
for successfully finishing this book.

 You're a star!

DK

Find the rhyme

Look at the first picture in each row, then draw
a ring around the picture that **rhymes** with it.

Copy these words by joining the dots.

cat

hat

cat   hat

Match the rhymes

Draw lines from the **van** to the things that **rhyme** with it.

Copy these words by joining the dots.

van  fan

van   fan

Odd one out

Look at the first picture in each row, then draw a ring around the picture that does **not rhyme** with it.

Copy these words by joining the dots.

ball  wall

ball wall

Join the rhymes

Draw a line joining each picture to the one that **rhymes** with it.

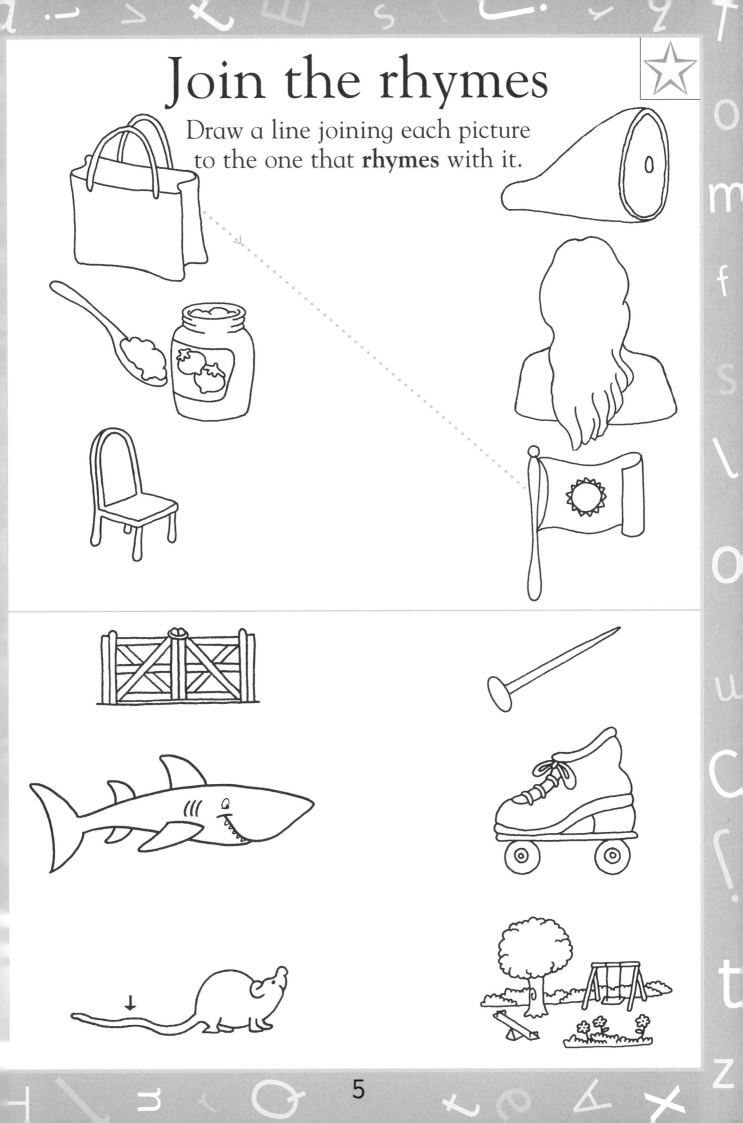

Find the rhyme

Look at the first picture in each row, then draw
a ring around the picture that **rhymes** with it.

Copy these words by joining the dots.

hen  ten

hen   ten

Match the rhymes

Draw lines from the **tree** to the things that **rhyme** with it.

Copy these words by joining the dots.

tree

bee

tree   bee

Odd ones out

Look at the first picture in each row, then draw (rings) around the pictures that do **not rhyme** with it.

Copy these words by joining the dots.

bell    shell

bell   shell

Join the rhymes

Draw a line joining each picture
to the one that **rhymes** with it.

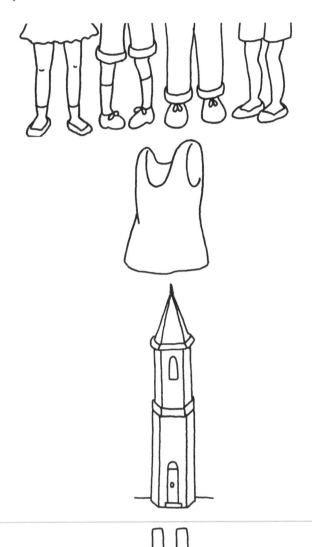

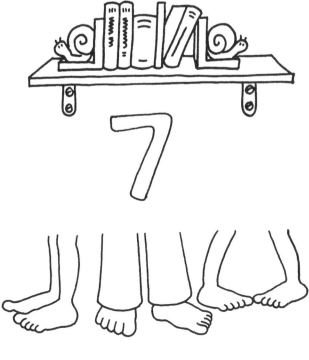

Find the rhyme

Look at the first picture in each row, then draw
a ring around the picture that **rhymes** with it.

  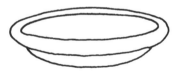 

Copy these words by joining the dots.

fish  dish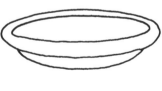

fish   dish

Match the rhymes

Draw lines from the **swing** to the things that **rhyme** with it.

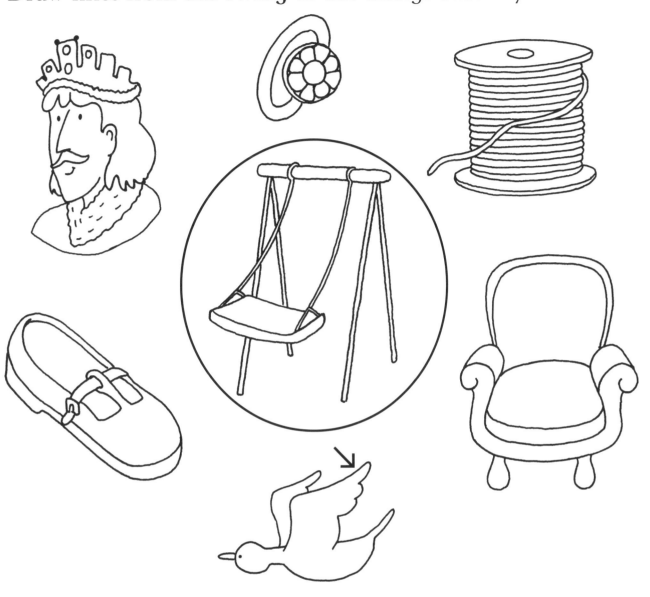

Copy these words by joining the dots.

wing   swing

ẅịṅg   ṡẅịṅg

Odd one out

Look at the first picture in each row, then draw a ring around the picture that does **not rhyme** with it.

Copy these words by joining the dots.

pie

cry

pie   cry

Join the rhymes

Draw a line joining each picture
to the one that **rhymes** with it.

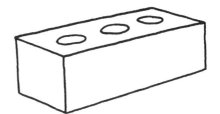

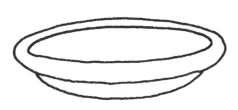

Odd ones out

Look at the first picture in each row, then draw rings around the pictures that do **not rhyme** with it.

Copy these words by joining the dots.

Match the rhymes

Draw lines from the **fox** to the things that **rhyme** with it.

Copy these words by joining the dots.

fox  socks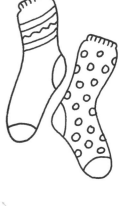

Odd one out

Look at the first picture in each row, then draw
a (ring) around the picture that does **not rhyme** with it.

Copy these words by joining the dots.

rose  toes

rose   toes

Join the rhymes

Draw a line joining each picture
to the one that **rhymes** with it.

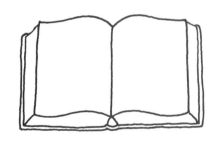

Find the rhyme

Look at the first picture in each row, then draw a ring around the picture that **rhymes** with it.

Copy these words by joining the dots.

hut

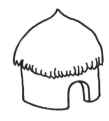

nut

hut   nut

Match the rhymes

Draw lines joining the **jug** to the things that **rhyme** with it.

Copy these words by joining the dots.

jug  mug

Odd one out

Look at the first picture in each row, then draw
a ring around the picture that does **not rhyme** with it.

Copy these words by joining the dots.

lump   hump

lump   hump

Join the rhymes

Draw a line joining each picture
to the one that **rhymes** with it.

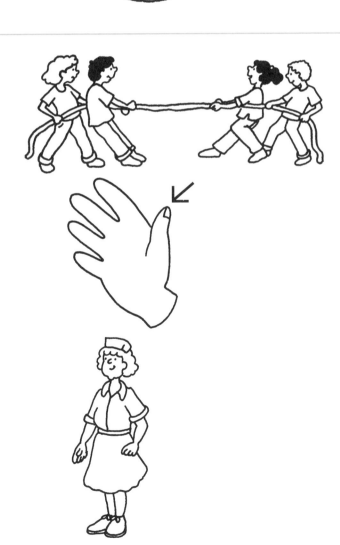

Draw it yourself

Draw something that **rhymes** with the picture in each row.

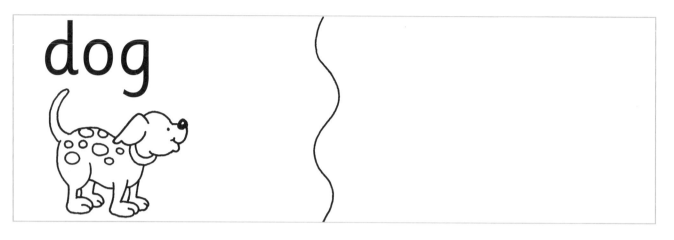

dog

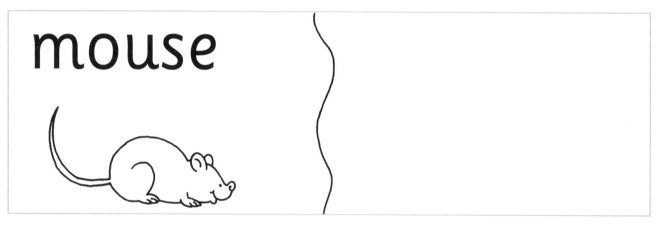

mouse

cat

hen

Draw it yourself

Draw something that **rhymes** with the picture in each row.

fox
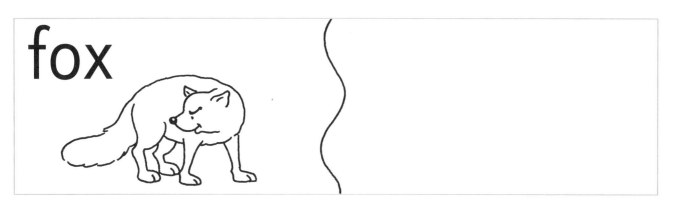

three
3
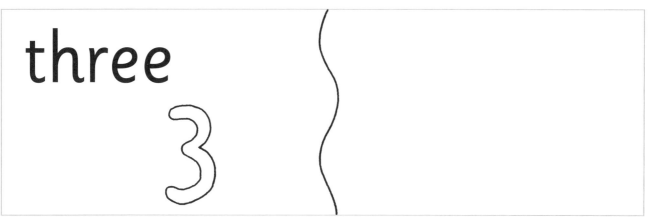

car
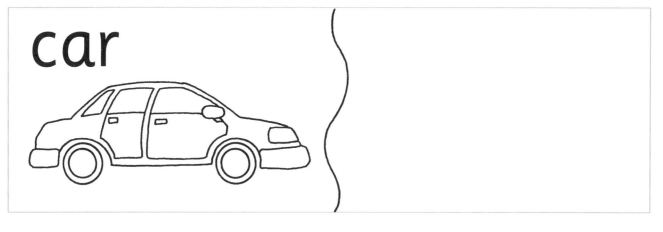

spoon
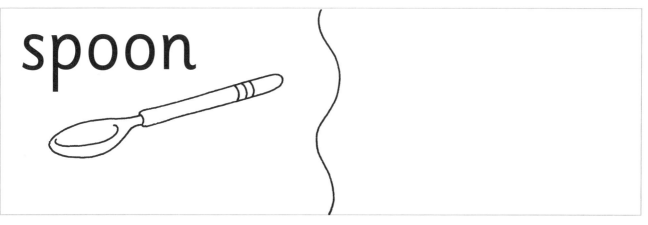

Find the pictures

Use a red pencil to colour the shapes around
the words that **rhyme** with in.

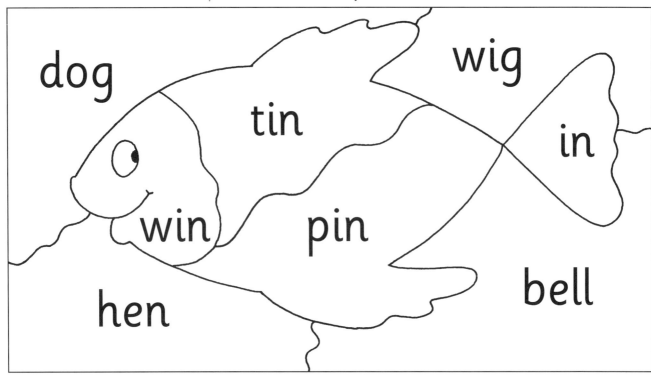

dog

wig

tin

in

win

pin

bell

hen

Use a blue pencil to colour the shapes around
the words that **rhyme** with ug.

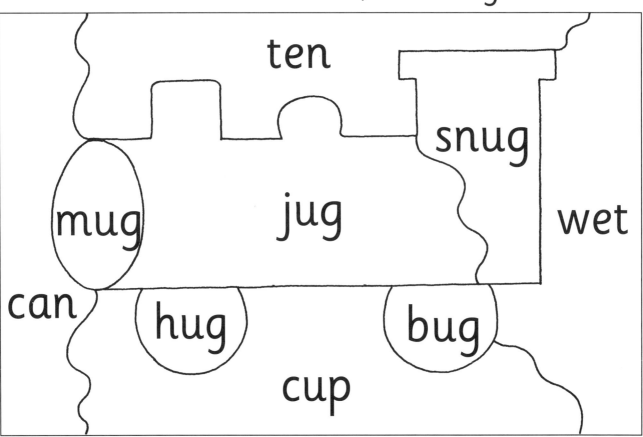

ten

snug

mug

jug

wet

can

hug

bug

cup

24

Find the pictures

Use a yellow pencil to colour the shapes around
the words that **rhyme** with ose.

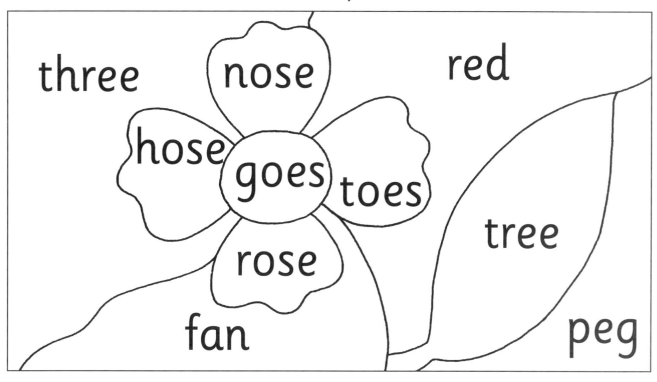

three — nose — red — hose — goes — toes — tree — rose — fan — peg

Use a green pencil to colour the shapes around
the words that **rhyme** with ell.

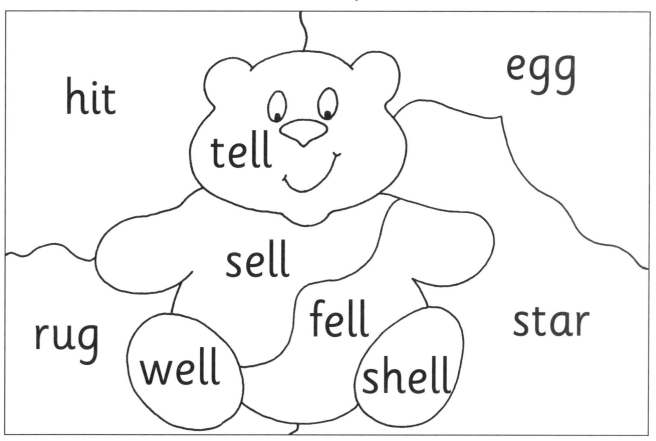

hit — egg — tell — sell — fell — star — rug — well — shell

Missing letters

Fill in the missing letter in the first box in each row.
Then write a **rhyming word** in the second box,
and draw a picture of it.

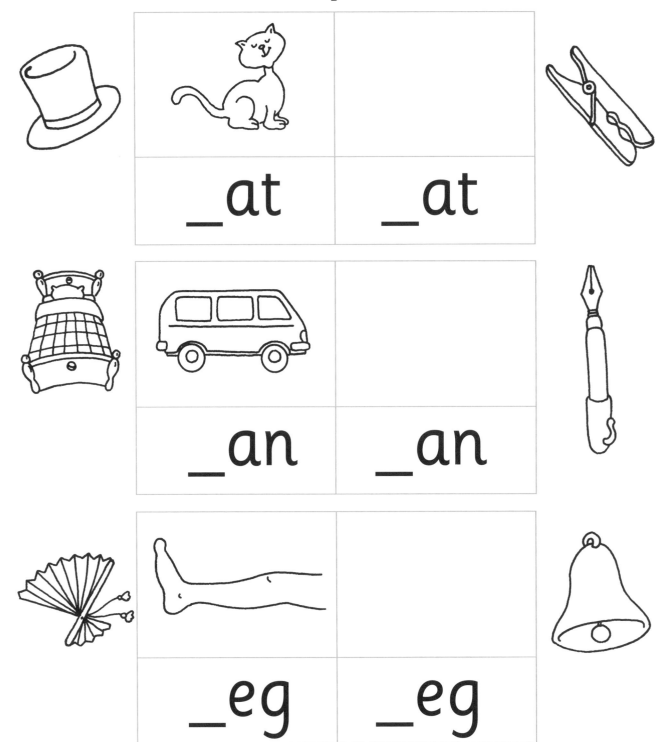

_at   _at

_an   _an

_eg   _eg

abcdefghijklmnopqrstuvwxyz

Missing letters

Fill in the missing letter in the first box in each row.
Then write a **rhyming word** in the second box,
and draw a picture of it.

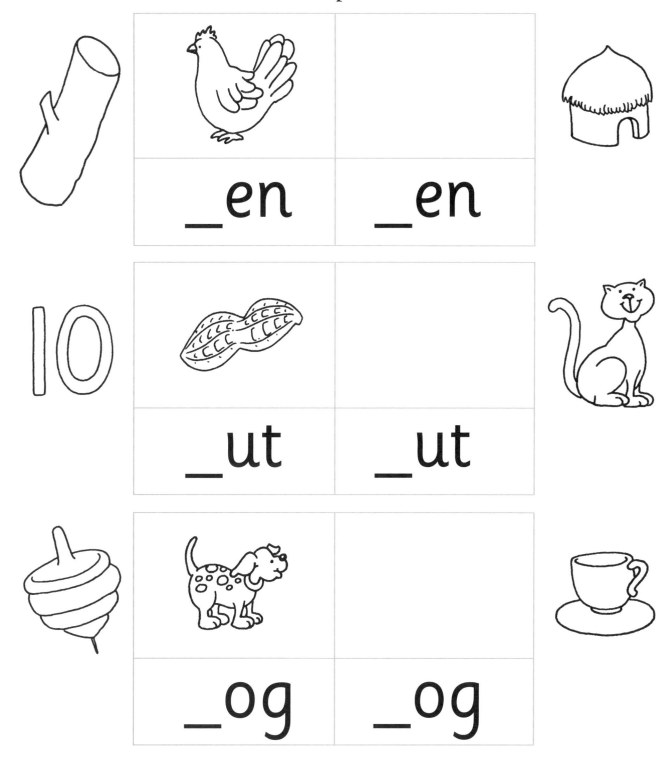

_en   _en

_ut   _ut

_og   _og

abcdefghijklmnopqrstuvwxyz

Missing letters

Fill in the missing letter in the first box in each row.
Then write a **rhyming word** in the second box,
and draw a picture of it.

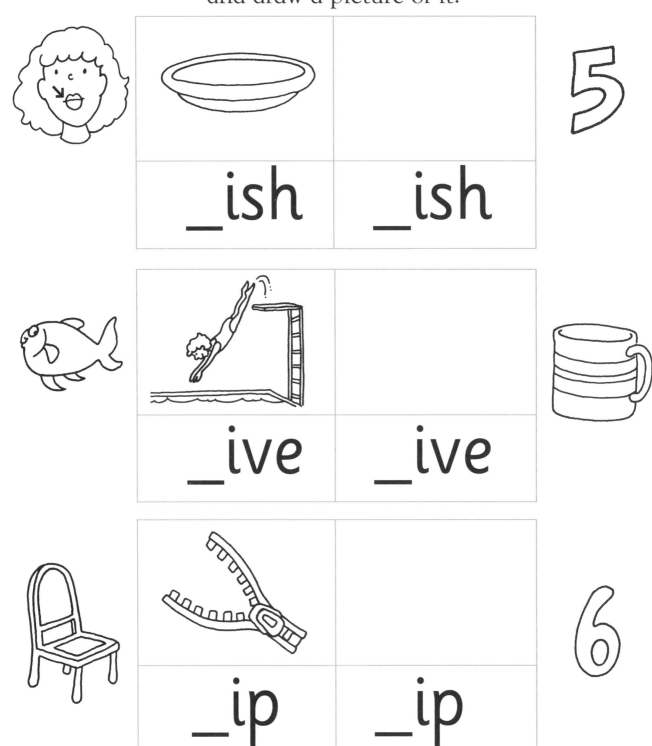

_ish   _ish

_ive   _ive

_ip   _ip

abcdefghijklmnopqrstuvwxyz

Missing letters

Fill in the missing letter in the first box in each row.
Then write a **rhyming word** in the second box,
and draw a picture of it.

_oat   _oat

_ell   _ell

_all   _all

abcdefghijklmnopqrstuvwxyz

A nursery rhyme

Finish each sentence by choosing the right **rhyming word** from the box below it. Write the word in the space.

1 2

One, two, buckle my _____.

| top | sock | shoe |

3 4

Three, four, knock at the _____.

| fin | door | floor |

5 6

Five, six, pick up _____.

| mix | fish | sticks |

More nursery rhymes

Finish each sentence by choosing the right **rhyming word** from the box below it. Write the word in the space.

Jack and Jill

went up the _____.

| hat | bell | hill |

One, two, three, four, five,

once I caught a fish _____.

| six | alive | fins |

Hickory, dickory, dock,

the mouse ran up the _____.

| dog | sock | clock |

Make up other words that **rhyme**.

Word puzzle

Look at the words at the bottom of the page.
First draw lines between the words that **rhyme**,
then find each word in the puzzle.

x	b	s	w	e	l	l
y	i	l	o	g	r	e
s	e	e	u	n	y	l
j	d	u	b	e	l	l
f	a	n	y	l	a	x
o	v	e	d	o	g	w
w	r	t	k	b	e	e
l	m	a	n	s	v	k

fan   well   see

      bee   log

dog   man   bell

Notes for Parents

This book is designed to help your child develop careful listening and early reading skills. Hearing and identifying rhyming words and making rhyming pairs are very important steps towards learning to read. Recent research shows that children with rhyming skills find it much easier to learn to read, write and spell in later years. The featured activities will encourage your child to match and sort rhyming pictures, to identify word patterns and to practise writing words with the same endings. Rhyming demands a lot of practice in listening carefully to how words sound, so enjoy spending time with your child thinking up silly rhymes together.

Content

By working through this book, your child will learn:
• to develop more refined listening skills;
• to identify similar sounds;
• to recognise word families and different word endings;
• to broaden his or her vocabulary;
• to develop an awareness of simple spelling;
• to develop eye-and-hand co-ordination;
• to practise handwriting skills;
• to write from left to right on the page;
• to write lower-case letters in the correct way.

How to help your child with rhyming

By singing and saying nursery rhymes with your child from a young age, you have been quite naturally introducing him or her to the enjoyment of rhyming words. Rhymes also have rhythm, as do many traditional stories, and this early exposure to rhythm and rhyme is very helpful to young children who are learning to read.

When choosing stories to read to your child, select those that have a strong rhythm or those that feature repeated phrases. For example, *The Little Red Hen* contains the phrases: *"Not I," said the cat, "Not I," said the dog* and *"Not I," said the pig*. Stories such as these are often fun to read aloud and will encourage your child to participate in storytelling.

When teaching rhymes and making up silly rhyming words with your child, it is important to be accurate at all times. For example, *ged, med* and *ked* are not real words, but they do rhyme. The words *nine* and *time* may sound very similar, but they do not rhyme.

Remember that some children find it difficult to hear an exact rhyme, especially if they have a cold. Others may have imprecise speech or have speech difficulties. In these cases, children may take a little longer to develop rhyming skills, so be patient and encourage their efforts.

How to use this book

Writing materials

Your child should have a pencil that is sharpened, but not too pointed. A soft lead pencil (2B) is preferable for the writing activities. If the pencil is too hard, your child's writing may be difficult to see on the page, which could lead to frustration.

As each activity involves colouring pictures, your child will need a range of colouring pencils or felt-tip pens – not the type that bleed through paper, as they will spoil subsequent pages. Avoid crayons, as these are likely to be too thick for accurately colouring the pictures, which could lead your child to become frustrated with his or her achievements.

Pencil grip

It is important to encourage your child to hold a pencil correctly. He or she should pick up a pencil in the dominant hand and hold it between the thumb and first finger. The second finger goes beneath the pencil to support it. Make sure that the pencil is not gripped too tightly and not held too close to the tip. It should rest between the first finger and the thumb at an angle of 45 degrees to the table. If your child has problems, it can help if you make a grip for the pencil using some Plasticine. Mould a small piece into a three-sided pyramid, and push the pencil through the middle – this will encourage your child to place his or her fingers correctly.

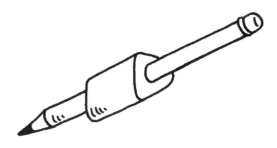 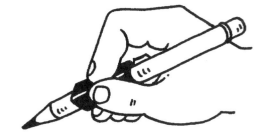

Getting the most from the activities

Always work through the book in page order. The book progresses from rhyming pictures to rhyming words and increases in difficulty. It is important not to miss out any of these stages as the contents have been carefully planned to take your child through a progression of rhyming and early reading and writing skills. If your child is struggling with the activities, don't worry. He or she may not be ready for this book or may only be able to do the first few activities. If this happens, leave the book for a while, and continue sharing rhymes and stories with your child. Later on, return to the book, recapping on any pages he or she may have already completed.

If your child has enjoyed a particular activity or is having some difficulty with it, try doing some additional practice on scrap paper. You may find it helpful to have some extra paper to hand before you start your activity sessions.

Working through the activities in this book should be an enjoyable shared experience for both you and your child, so choose a moment when you have time to concentrate and your child is not too tired or hungry. Sit together and read the instructions aloud. Make sure that your child understands what he or she is expected to do for each activity.

Don't spend too long on each activity session – it's better to keep it short and fun and to let your child get a feel for the rhyming and listening skills involved. Celebrate your child's success, and build his or her confidence by giving plenty of praise and encouragement along the way.

Page-by-page notes

page 2

Page 2 – Find the rhyme

This activity is based on the vowel *a* and features words in the "at" word family. For each exercise, say together the names of all the pictures in that row. Then ask your child to name the first picture on the left of the page again and to draw a ring around the picture that rhymes with it. The two rhyming words at the bottom of the page have been selected for your child to copy. When writing rounded letters, make sure that your child always starts at the top and draws in an anti-clockwise direction.

Page 3 – Match the rhymes

This activity is based on the vowel *a* and features words in the "an" word family. First say together the names of all the pictures. Next, your child has to find all the pictures that rhyme with the one in the centre of the page. If a picture rhymes, draw a line to link it up. Once again, your child can copy the rhyming words at the bottom of the page. If your child is ready, point out that the letter endings are the same. Talk about the sound that this pair of letters makes, and explain that new words are made when a different letter sound is added at the start of a word.

page 3

Page 4 – Odd one out

This activity is based on the vowel *a* and features examples of several word families. The task on this page is to identify the picture that does not rhyme with the first picture on the left of the page. Say together the names of all the pictures. Encourage your child to listen and hear the different sounds. Handwriting practice using rhymes from the "all" word family is provided at the bottom of the page.

page 4

Page 5 – Join the rhymes

This activity is based on the vowel *a* and also contains examples of several word families. Say together the names of all the pictures. Ask your child to match the pictures on the left with those that rhyme on the right. Encourage your child to draw each linking line from the left to the right-hand side of the page. This will help to reinforce the correct writing movement.

page 5

Pages 6 and 7 – Find the rhyme and Match the rhymes

These activities are based on the vowel *e* and feature words in the "en" and "ee" word families. Say together the names of the pictures. On page 6, ask your child to draw a ring around the picture in each row that rhymes with the first one on the left. On the next page, ask your child to find all the pictures that rhyme with the one in the centre of the page and to draw linking lines. Handwriting practice is provided at the bottom of both pages.

pages 6 and 7

Pages 8 and 9 – Odd ones out and Join the rhymes

These activities are based on the vowel *e* and feature examples of several word families. On page 8, say together the name of each picture aloud and encourage your child to listen to and hear the different sounds. Then ask him or her to identify the pictures that do not rhyme with the first picture on the left. Handwriting practice using rhymes from the "ell" word family is provided at the bottom of the page. On page 9, ask your child to match the pictures on the left with those that rhyme on the right. Encourage him or her to draw linking lines from left to right.

pages 8 and 9

Pages 10 and 11 – Find the rhyme and Match the rhymes

These activities are based on the vowel *i* and feature examples of several word families. Your child has to draw a ring around the picture in each row that rhymes with the first one on the left. Next, your child has to find all the pictures that rhyme with the one in the centre of the page and draw linking lines. Handwriting practice is provided at the bottom of both pages.

pages 10 and 11

Pages 12 and 13 – Odd one out and **Join the rhymes**

These activities are based on the vowel *i* and feature examples of several word families. Your child has to ring the picture that does not rhyme with the first picture on the left of the page. Handwriting practice is provided for two words that rhyme but do not have the same spelling (*pie* and *cry*). Talk about this, emphasising that some words still sound the same even though they don't look the same. On page 13, your child has to match the pictures on the left with those that rhyme on the right by drawing linking lines.

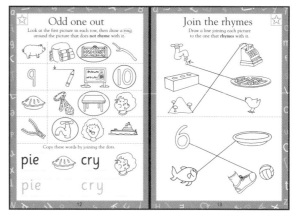

pages 12 and 13

Pages 14 and 15 – Odd ones out and **Match the rhymes**

These activities are based on the vowel *o* and feature examples of several word families. The task is to identify the pictures in each row that do not rhyme with the first picture on the left of the page. There is handwriting practice using rhymes from the "oon" word family. On page 15, ask your child to find the pictures that rhyme with the one in the centre of the page and to draw linking lines. There is handwriting practice for two words that rhyme but do not have the same spelling (*fox* and *socks*).

pages 14 and 15

Pages 16 and 17 – Odd one out and **Join the rhymes**

These activities are also based mainly on the vowel *o*. Ask your child to ring the picture that does not rhyme with the first picture on the left of the page. There is handwriting practice for two words that rhyme but do not have the same spelling (*rose* and *toes*). On page 17, your child matches the pictures on the left with those that rhyme on the right by drawing linking lines.

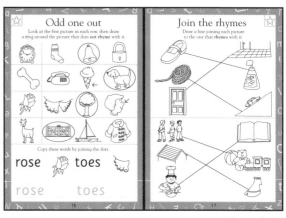

pages 16 and 17

Pages 18 and 19 – Find the rhyme and Match the rhymes

These activities are based on the vowel *u* and feature examples of several word families. On page 18, ask your child to ring the picture in each row that rhymes with the first one on the left. On page 19, ask your child to find all the pictures that rhyme with the one in the centre and to draw linking lines. Handwriting practice is provided at the bottom of both pages.

Pages 20 and 21 – Odd one out and Join the rhymes

These activities are based mainly on the vowel *u* and feature examples of several word families. On page 20, ask your child to ring the picture in each row that does not rhyme with the first picture on the left. On page 21, help your child match the pictures on the left with those that rhyme on the right by drawing linking lines.

Pages 22 and 23 – Draw it yourself

These activities introduce written words with the picture illustrations. Ask your child to draw his or her own picture of something that rhymes with each word. If your child finds it difficult to think of rhyming words, have fun making up words, however silly, until your child discovers a rhyme that can be illustrated. Alternatively, look back at earlier pages to refresh your child's memory.

Pages 24 and 25 – Find the pictures

These activities have hidden pictures. Say together all the words aloud. Your child has to find all the words in a particular word family and colour them either red, blue, yellow or green to reveal the mystery picture. Choose other colours to finish the rest of the pictures.

pages 18 and 19

pages 20 and 21

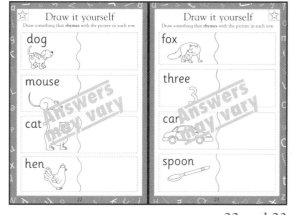

pages 22 and 23

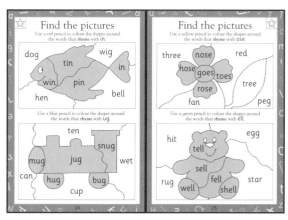

pages 24 and 25

Pages 26, 27, 28 and 29 – Missing letters

To help with the activities on the next four pages, ask your child to say the first word ending aloud and then to fill in the box on the left. Next, your child can either find and copy the rhyming picture from around the border of the page, or think up another rhyming word to use instead. The alphabet is printed at the bottom of the page to remind your child of the different letter shapes.

pages 28 and 29

Pages 30 and 31 – A nursery rhyme and More nursery rhymes

These nursery rhymes have missing words for your child to fill in. Say together the rhymes and the words in the boxes. Your child should listen to the sounds of the words and look at the word endings to find the word that completes each rhyme. As an extra clue, lines are used to indicate the number of letters in each missing word.

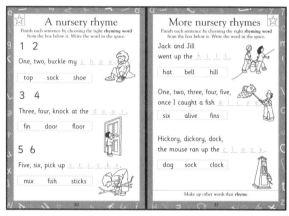

pages 30 and 31

Page 32 – Word puzzle

Help your child find the pairs of rhyming words at the bottom of the page. Your child should draw a line linking the rhyming words and then find each word, one by one, among the letters in the word square. Encourage your child to draw a ring around each word as it is found. If this activity is too difficult for your child at a first attempt, put it to one side and return to it later. In the meantime, have fun exploring rhymes.

page 32